Spiritual
Lightning Rods
Connected to the Father of Lights!

Edie Bayer

DEDICATED

Mom and Dad, who saw me through those tough early years.
And then again in those tough later years.
Thank you for choosing Jesus!
And Thank You for praying me into the Kingdom!

Because of You.

CONTENTS

EDIE BAYER

Preface

The year was 2006. God started talking to me about a book I was going to write. I had just read Psalm 16 verses 7-9, and He started to stir inside me, speaking to me about writing it.

I honestly forgot about it for years, then suddenly, there it was again!

> **7 I will bless the Lord, Who has given me counsel;**
>
> **Yes, my heart instructs me in the night seasons.**
>
> **8 I have set the Lord continually before me;**
>
> **Because He is at my right hand,**
>
> **I shall not be moved.**
>
> **9 Therefore my heart is glad and my glory [my inner self] rejoices;**
>
> **My body too shall rest *and* confidently dwell in safety.**

I found a note that I had written about it from way back then, and it all came flooding back. I wasn't even writing books at that time! I was just a struggling single Mom living in a single wide trailer with my son, working and going to church and trying to figure out how to walk with the Lord. Holy Spirit informed me personally about it, a prophecy straight from God! I even knew then to break down each of the verses into chapters, just like God has done in this book.

A few weeks went past after I found that note, and the Lord reminded me I had to write this book from way back then. I couldn't even remember the number of the Psalm. Honestly, I couldn't remember if it was a Psalm or a Proverb! But Holy Spirit brought it back to my remembrance.

The mind-boggling part of this whole experience is that God told me in 2006 that one day I would write this book. In December of 2013 I wrote a blog entry which is now Chapter 1 of this book. It has taken me several weeks at least to write this book. During this time period I have completely forgotten what was in each chapter, since God is doing all the writing!

When I finished Chapter 7 tonight, I went back to begin the arduous task of editing the book beginning in Chapter 1. Halfway down the page I started crying, because God wrote the last chapter in December 2013.

Read it and you'll see what I mean.

It was 7 years between the time that God told me to write this book and the time He wrote the last chapter.

7 years ago! Completion! That's Powerful!

CHAPTER 1:

I WILL BLESS THE LORD
WHO HAS GIVEN ME COUNSEL

There is tremendous POWER in taking your counsel from the Lord. I have learned the hard way to ask God FIRST! Sometimes when we meet He gives instruction, sometimes direction, sometimes reprimand or chastising, but always counsel. Sometimes He just loves on me! But I LOVE when He reveals something about Himself to me through divine revelation!

Here is a page from my blog, "God's Notes", where He revealed something about Himself to me in Psalm 16.

This is a sure word of revelation from the Most High, downloaded through his Spiritual Lightning Rod!

Pay attention to what God is HIGHLIGHTING to you right now!!

God put me in Psalm 16 this morning. I love the first verse, "Keep and protect me, O God, for in You I have found refuge...and in You do I put my trust and hide myself." (Psalm 16:1, Amp.)

As I was reading it the second time, He drew my attention to the number itself, "16". He asked me, "What does that look like?"

I knew He meant using Hebrew letters. So I did a little research online, and interestingly enough, the Hebrew pictographs are "added unto" each other, similar to the way we do in the United States in our "base ten" system by adding 10 + (whatever number) to come up with a figure.

However, they do it a little differently....i.e., 9 + 7. The reason is because if they use the Hebrew pictographs for the numbers 10 + 6 *it's another way of saying the name of the Lord!*

Then the Lord asked me, "What is the definition of 'Psalm'?"

In my head I knew it was a song or a poem...but He knew that I knew that, which means that there was a deeper meaning. So, I looked up the etymology of the word itself, PSALM. It comes from a Greek root word which means "to pull" or "to pluck". Immediately, I thought of "pulling my heart strings!"

I then knew what the Lord was saying. When we DRAW ON (pull on, or pluck ---*Psalm*) the NAME of the LORD (16)....He keeps and protects us. We find our refuge in Him, and in Him we put our trust and hide

ourselves.   He wants us to draw on His Name, to pull
on His power, in the Name of Jesus...Yeshua.

Read the Word out loud. It's powerful to make
declarations in His Name.

The Hebrew numeric system operates on the additive
principle in which the numeric values of the letters are
added together to form the total. For example, 177 is
represented as קעז which corresponds to 100 + 70 + 7 =
177.

Mathematically, this type of system requires 27 letters
(1-9, 10-90, 100-900). In practice the last letter, *tav*
(which has the value 400) is used in combination with
itself and/or other letters from *kof* (100) onwards, to
generate numbers from 500 and above. Alternatively,
the 22-letter Hebrew numeral set is sometimes
extended to 27 by using 5 *sofit* (final) forms of the
Hebrew letters.

Key exceptions

By convention, the numbers 15 and 16 are
represented as □ו"ט□ 9(+ 6) and □ז"ט□ (9 + 7),
respectively. This is done in order to refrain from using
the two-letter combinations ה־י □(10 + 5)□ and ו־י □(10
+ 6)□ (which are alternate written forms for the Name
of God) in everyday writing. In the calendar, this
manifests every full moon, since all Hebrew months
start on a new moon.

Combinations which would spell out words with
negative connotations are sometimes avoided by
switching the order of the letters. For instance,

□תשמ"ד□ (meaning "you/it will be destroyed") might instead be written as □תשד"מ□ or ד"שמת (meaning "end to demon"). (1)

Word History

The Greek word *psallein* originally meant "to pull" or "to pluck." It then came to be used with the meaning "to play a stringed musical instrument." From this verb came the noun *psalmos,* which literally meant "the twanging of a harp." Since harp music often accompanied singing, *psalmos* took on the meaning of "a song sung to harp music" and later simply "a song or poem." It was borrowed into Latin as *psalmus* and came into English as *psalm.* (2)

CHAPTER 2:

YES, MY HEART INSTRUCTS ME
IN THE NIGHT SEASONS

This can only mean one thing to me, and that is
DREAM INTERPRETATION. Dream Interpretation is a
POWERFUL weapon! Few people know the intricacies
and intimacies of Dream Interpretation. You should
be one of them!

God never ceases to speak, and a lot of it happens
during the hours when we are sleeping! When we are
asleep there is no wall to block what the Lord has to
say to us, and His message gets right through.

When the Lord initially told me I would write a book
based on this Psalm I hadn't learned anything about
Christian Dream Interpretation yet. I hadn't even met
the person who would lead me to it, the one the Lord
would use who would spark my interest in doing it.

That divine encounter was still months away.

The book of Job says it best, in 33:14-17 (AMP) ---

"¹⁴ For God [does reveal His will; He] speaks not only once, but more than once, even though men do not regard it [including you, Job].

¹⁵ [One may hear God's voice] in a dream, in a vision of the night, when deep sleep falls on men while slumbering upon the bed,

¹⁶ Then He opens the ears of men and seals their instruction [terrifying them with warnings],

¹⁷ That He may withdraw man from his purpose and cut off pride from him [disgusting him with his own disappointing self-sufficiency]."

My dream interpretation journey began in McAllen, Texas on a missions trip. During the day the group of people I went with sat at the feet of an instructor, and at night we went across the border to minister in Mexico. God set me up for success in Dream Interpretation, and later prophetic interpretation, because He deliberately caused me to take a class that would change my destiny! The Apostle teaching the class, Dr. Terry Thompson, was speaking about symbolism in the bible. I had never heard of this before! I was intrigued.

After class I asked him what the best book was on the subject, and he told me about Kevin J. Conner's "Interpreting the Symbols and Types" book. I remember being interested in the topic, but I didn't get the book at that time.

I was talking to one of the church leaders later about dream interpretation, and she handed me a copy of Kathy Gabler's "Getting to the Heart of Dreams". She told me I could read it but asked me to return the book, because it belonged to her husband. Mr. Kent, if you ever read this, I still have your book! It's well-worn, but you can have it back!

A year or two later I met a man who had just started his own dream interpretation journey. We talked about dreams, and their interpretation, and various tools we had available to us to use. My list was short! That is when I bought a couple of dream interpretation cards by John Paul Jackson's "Streams" ministries, then graduated to his entire 5-cd package, a huge expenditure for me back then. But I was hooked! I had to have tools to dissect these puzzles from God!

From there I started researching dream interpretation tools in earnest. The best book I have found on Dream Interpretation, encyclopedia style anyway, is Ira Milligan's, "Understanding the Dreams You Dream". This book is invaluable in deciphering dreams for beginners, and it is still the first book I turn to when I have a dream I need help interpreting. I bought a used copy of it online, and finally got the book Dr. Terry Thompson had told me about years earlier, Kevin J. Conner's "Interpreting the Symbols and Types"! These two tools, along with the Streams Ministries information and Kathy Gabler's book, were the tools in my workshed to dissect and interpret the puzzles God gives us each night.

Within the last year I added some of Barbie Breathitt's spiral bound card sets to my now full-grown library of dream interpretation information. In the last few years I have bought a couple more books by different authors, but the books listed here are the foundation for my dream interpretation skills.

Except for Holy Spirit!! Without Him I wouldn't be able to interpret a paper grocery bag while I was still in the store! Lots of times I rely solely on Holy Spirit for the interpretation of a dream, because many times God will use symbols custom-tailored to the individuals' life. As an example, I do not particularly care for dogs. My husband loves them! So, a dog in a dream would mean something completely different for him than for me, since he would view a dog as a friend or companion, and I would view one as a nuisance or an aggravation.

As an example, recently I was speaking with a woman whose daughter had recently died. She said she had a dream of her fully grown daughter in a shower, holding a baby. The baby slipped and started to go down the drain. This woman tried to save the baby, but couldn't stop it from going down the drain.

All the dream interpretation skills I have ever learned tell me that a baby is a new ministry or new life. A shower is always cleansing in one's life. However, Holy Spirit let me know immediately this interpretation was a little different. Since her daughter had so recently passed on, this dream was interpreted to mean that God was trying to cleanse her of the guilty thought process that she might have been able to do something about it, to stop her daughter (her "baby") from dying, somehow thinking that she could help save her life from "going down the drain".

Another dream my husband had recently was a rooster pulling our cat on a half-bale of hay, with a smaller white chicken behind it. In his dream my husband looked at the rooster and said, "What a good rooster!"

This would be a pizza dream for you, but in our world, we raise chickens! So, the interpretation was very easy. My husband is the sole provider in our household, aside from the little bit we get from selling the eggs and some of the chickens, our boarder here at the house and my part-time ministry income. On the farm, everything has to "pull its own weight", meaning it must support itself in some way – either as food or by selling it or its by-products.

Jesus broke down the parable of the sower, one symbol at a time in Matthew 13 when He described it to His disciples. That is how I learned to interpret dreams, symbol by symbol. So, in this dream, my husband was the rooster. The hay is provision. I was the cat, sitting on the half-bale of hay (or "half-pay", since we live on only one income), being pulled by the rooster.

His dream means that I am NOT "pulling my own weight" -- HE is pulling me!! The smaller white chicken behind me is the income from the farm, our "chicken money" as we call it. He looked at the rooster and said, "What a good rooster!" This dream is a snap-shot of a moment in time of his life, a thought process. God was sounding the depths of his heart. In this dream, he was doing a good thing as a husband, supporting both his wife and the farm, pulling everyone's weight on half-income. And I am along for the ride!

If you look up roosters in dream interpretation, they are generally indicative of "pride". This is NOT my husband. Darryl WORKS at being humble. He is a very humble man, so it would take Holy Spirit to interpret this dream accurately. Cats are attitudes, mindsets or paradigms. They can also stand for independence or willfulness, depending on the dream. However, in this dream I know I am the cat, because I am sitting on the hay being pulled by my husband, the rooster.

Think about it this way: we have three cats. They don't really DO anything! I suppose they keep the mice at bay, but besides that, they have no other job except to primp, play, eat and sleep. They are nice to snuggle with and they will let you pet them sometimes, if they are in the mood. But other than that....they truly are just along for the ride!

Whether it was God congratulating him and telling him what a good husband (rooster) he is, or if he was merely patting himself on the back in his dream I do not know. I do know that Holy Spirit gave me the interpretation of this dream based on our unique individual circumstances of farm life and single income living. Now, what God wants Darryl to DO with that information is between Him and Darryl.

I know it gave me a cutesy phrase to use with my husband. I now tell him, "What a good rooster!"

Another dream interpretation came when I was in South Dakota ministering at a church there. A group of us, the Glory Five, had invited the congregation to give us their dreams for interpretation on the spot.

First up was a man who had a dream that he had two piles of corn on the ground by a trailer. A turkey had come up onto one of the piles of corn and was eating it. A skunk came into the picture and sprayed at him, but there was an invisible wall that protected him that would not let the skunk spray come through.

Being a "farm person" myself, this was a no-brainer for me. Note: That is why God talked to Farmers about sowing and reaping, and Fishermen about boats and fishing. They could RELATE!

I interpreted the dream on the spot, beginning at the end of the dream, and working my way backward into the interpretation. I explained first of all that the invisible wall was God protecting him from the "stinky" thing that was coming. Even though the skunk DID spray, it didn't get on him because he was protected! The turkey was something that was coming to "eat" what he had laid up. Initially I did not get an interpretation on the trailer, but one of the other girls said that it meant that he was able to move into another field, so to speak. I interpreted it as a warning dream in which the Lord was telling him in advance that some stink was getting ready to occur, but that He would protect this man.

Following the interpretation we learned from him that he was a former Pastor-turned-farmer who was looking at going back to the church!

There is POWER in dream interpretation. God speaks to us continually. If you don't already, begin to journal your dreams. Get a good resource to help you interpret your dreams. And pray into them. Holy Spirit is the best dream interpreter in this earth realm. Rely on His Power!

CHAPTER 3:

I HAVE SET THE LORD CONTINUALLY BEFORE ME.

You're in Control. You have the POWER.

The King James Bible translation says, **"I have set the LORD always before me."** The Message says, **"Day and night I'll stick with GOD."** The Amplified says it in this chapter's title, **"I have set the Lord continually before me."**

Whatever version you are reading, YOU must do it. All of the versions I have read have translated this phrase to say "I HAVE (done it)....". It doesn't say God did it, or that it was luck, or chance, or the weather or Mother Earth, or one day you will wake up and find yourself "the perfect Christian" smack-dab in the middle of God's perfect will.

Every single bible version I have read says that YOU have to do it. It's not a very laid back way to live, is it? This is an action phrase. You must do something to keep the Lord in your sights, day and night. What is that something? What did David do to keep the Lord continually in front of him, at the front of his mind and his thoughts, his heart, ergo his actions?

Prayer.

See, God is real. David knew this. God was WITH him. God and David had a thing, a really personal thing going on, a real relationship. David talked to God constantly. I don't know if he heard an audible voice, or if he "felt/heard" like most of us the sound of the voice of God from deep within. But he was in CONSTANT COMMUNICATION with God.

The Word says, **"Draw near to God and He will draw near to you."** (James 4:8, ESV) God is an "If, Then" God. That means God says, "If you, Then I..." It means you must do something, then God will do something.

The funny thing is He gives us the rules! He tells us if we do a certain thing, this is the result we can expect. In this case, YOU must draw near first, THEN He will draw near to you.

Let's look at Deuteronomy 8:6-9 for another example in the Amplified version of the Bible:

6 "So you shall keep the commandments of the Lord your God, to walk in His ways and [reverently] fear Him."

Remember, God is an "If, Then" God. If you do something, He will do something. So, there's the instruction, what YOU must do. You must keep His commandments and reverence Him.

Now here is the response from God, what HE will do.

⁷ "For the Lord your God is bringing you into a good land, a land of brooks of water, of fountains and springs, flowing forth in valleys and hills;

⁸ A land of wheat and barley, and vines and fig trees and pomegranates, a land of olive trees and honey;

⁹ A land in which you shall eat food without shortage and lack nothing in it; a land whose stones are iron and out of whose hills you can dig copper."

Did you notice the *goodness* of the things He will do for you, once you do something for Him? He is always like that!

Things not going so well for you? Check your "Fear Factor" --- your Fear of the Lord! Are you keeping His commandments and reverencing the Lord as He requires? The fear of the Lord is the beginning of wisdom! (Prov. 9:10)

His Word is pretty specific. But here is an actual "If, Then" example where God actually SAYS the "If you, Then I":

"So _IF_ you faithfully obey the commands I am giving you today – to love the LORD your God and to serve him with all your heart and with all your

soul – _THEN_ I will send rain on your land in its season, both autumn and spring rains, so that you may gather in your grain, new wine and oil. I will provide grass in the fields for your cattle, and you will eat and be satisfied." (Deuteronomy 11:13-15, emphasis mine)

See what I mean? YOUR ACTIONS ARE YOUR SEED. God spoke and Light WAS. His WORD was His Seed. (Boy that will preach!) He needed nothing more than His Word to create something out of nothingness. However, even though Jesus is the Son of God wrapped up in an earth-suit, in this earthly realm Jesus still had to have something in His hand, A SEED, i.e.; the mud and His spit on the blind man's eyes. Then of course he needed the loaves and the fish.

Jesus speaks of Himself repeatedly as the "Son of Man". So are WE also sons of men. We have Holy Spirit wrapped up in an earth suit, just as God Himself was wrapped up in flesh. That means that we need something, too -- A SEED. Thankfully, God has already given it to us.

Its US.

That's it, just US. It's You. It's Me. We have to crawl up on the altar and present ourselves as a living sacrifice (every day!).

But more than our physical bodies God wants our HEART, our Soul and our Spirit. He wants our mind, will and emotions, the total man. God wants us to speak and see what we say. In order for that to happen, we must FIRST give ourselves to God. So, in order for us to keep Him continually before us, we must give Him something first – US. Our hearts. Our minds, our attitudes. Our finances. In short, Everything.

We ARE that seed.

But honestly, no one can do all things at one time. And no one expects you to, certainly not the Lord. I've heard it said that if God gave us the scrubbing that we needed all at once that we wouldn't survive it! Your new life is more like an onion – peeling off layer after layer of dead skin until we get to the soft, new flesh.

You will need to slowly adapt to this new level of thinking, this new life. Yes, we are new creatures in Christ. But we need to break out of our chrysalis of the old man to become the new creation, the butterfly. That doesn't happen overnight for the caterpillar, either!! On average, it takes 2-24 weeks for a caterpillar to turn into a butterfly. That is as much as 6-months for a creature that survives for only a month in the wild in its new form.

Consider Jesus. He was 30 when He began His ministry. He died on the cross at 33. That means that Jesus was in His chrysalis for 30 years! He trained, virtually unknown and "in the dark", for 30 years. He came into the public eye at 30 and for 3-years ministered publicly, out in the open, a butterfly.

Think about it. Jesus began His new "career" with a miracle at the wedding at Cana. That was a life-changing event! A LIFE TRANSFORMING EVENT, if you will, when He stepped out of obscurity into destiny. However, it was when He was baptized by John, and the Holy Spirit came upon Him as a Dove, that His true ministry began.

Jesus constantly kept the Father before Him. He was in constant contact with the Father, fasting and praying.

So we have come full circle, beginning and ending with prayer. Jesus prayed constantly. And so you also have a need to pray constantly, to stay in constant communication with the Father, through Holy Spirit.

There is POWER in prayer!

Prayer will keep the Lord continually before you. For all eternity!

Amen!

CHAPTER 4:

BECAUSE HE IS AT MY RIGHT HAND

The Right Hand is the Hand of POWER.

The Bible speaks in many, many places about the "right hand of God", and Jesus being at "the right hand of the Father".

For those of you that don't know this yet, you and I are in two places right now, both here on earth and seated with Jesus in Heaven. Because we have Holy Spirit IN US, indwelling in us, we can simultaneously be in two places at the same time. That puts us at God's Right Hand, also.

Need scripture? You should! Ephesians 2:6 says in the Amplified Bible,
"And He raised us up together with Him and made

us sit down together [giving us *joint seating with Him*] in the heavenly sphere [by virtue of our being] in Christ Jesus (the Messiah, the Anointed One)."

The Aramaic Bible in Plain English says it a little more clearly,

"And he has raised us up with him and *seated us with himself* in Heaven in Yeshua The Messiah."

AMEN!!

So, we are at God's right hand. But doesn't this scripture, our chapter heading, say that God is at our right hand?

Yes. We are at the right hand of Jesus, who is at the right hand of the Father. We are at the Father's Right Hand, and He is at ours, because we are at the Right Hand of Jesus. Think of a circle, where everybody is to your right, and you are at everybody else's right!

In view of the POWER and AUTHORITY of being on the Right Hand of God, it is a position of honor for us. We ARE honored. We are Kings and Priests! After all, a King died for you! How much more honored could you be than that?

To be seated on the Right Hand of the host at the supper table in Bible days was the PROMINENT position, the position of importance, where the dignitaries, honored guests and celebrities sat. Ok, and the religious people, too, who made themselves important in their own hearts and heads. Jesus is seated at the right hand of the Father, a place of honor that speaks to his authority as God.

"Looking away [from all that will distract] to Jesus, Who is the Leader *and* the Source of our faith [giving the first incentive for our belief] and is also its Finisher [bringing it to maturity and perfection]. He, for the joy [of obtaining the prize] that was set before Him, endured the cross, despising *and* ignoring the shame, and is now seated at the right hand of the throne of God." (Hebrews 12:2, Amplified)

Now, if you are a right handed man, you keep your wallet in your right hip or right front pocket of your pants. That makes it easy to find it and take it out. It is at your right hand.

If you are right handed, you typically will keep things to your right, to make them convenient and easy to pull out or lift up, right? RIGHT. So, God being at your right hand makes Him convenient to turn toward as He is always close by and at the ready. Keeping Him close by and at the ready makes Him your POWER.

Using Conner's book, "Interpreting the Types and Symbols", we can find the symbol of the "hand" defined as, "Symbol of strength, power, action, possession." (3) How much more so when it is the Lord's hand?

The connection between POWER and God's arm and hand is evident in scripture. (All references below are American King James Version).

"You have a mighty arm; Strong is Your hand, and high is Your right hand." (Psalm 89:13)

"Your right hand, O LORD, has dashed the enemy in pieces." (Exodus 15:6)

"But it was Your right hand, Your arm, and the light of Your countenance." (Psalm 44:3)

"Your right hand is full of righteousness." (Psalm 48:10)

"Awake, awake, put on strength, O Arm of the LORD!" (Isaiah 51:9)

"Behold, the Lord GOD shall come with a strong hand, And His arm shall rule for Him." (Isaiah 40:10)

*"A "right hand man" is not someone who is always at a person's right hand. Rather it means someone who is **a chief assistant or strong supporter**. To sit at the right hand of someone is **symbolic of being very close to them, indispensable, useful, and honored**, like the youngest child of Jacob, named Benjamin or "Son of the Right Hand."—Whatthebiblesays.com* (4)

The bottom line is that God is your Power Source. He is always ready, always available, at your Right Hand. He is your chief assistant and strong supporter! He is VERY close to you, indispensable, useful and honored. He is close by and at the ready. He is the Power on your right hand!

CHAPTER 5:

I SHALL NOT BE MOVED!

It is easy see power when you witness a racecar zipping around a track at 200 miles per hour. It's also just as easy to see the power in a cheetah travelling across the plains at 70 miles per hour. It's very easy to see power in a bulldozer! It's also just as easy to see the power in the muscles bulging under an athlete's Tee-shirt.

But what about something that doesn't move?

There is power in stability. If you think of a bull dog with its short, stocky legs set in place, it is immovable. That's POWER! The foundation for a building is dug down deeply and largely hidden underground, giving a building the power, the strength and stability it needs, resulting in a structure that will withstand the elements and the test of time.

That's YOU. You are the bulldog. God is your legs set in place, immovable. He is the POWER! You are the building. God is your foundation, hidden and strong. God is your stability. He is your Strong Tower, He is your Shelter, He is your shield and your buckler. He is the mighty, impenetrable fortress. He is God and beside Him there is no other. He is your POWER!

When you see someone who is "double-minded", as in the book of James, one who is tossed to and fro by every wind of doctrine, it's easy to see his instability. We might view this as a weakness, and wonder why he doesn't know what he believes!

When you stand in one place, not moving anywhere, you are stable. That's POWERFUL.

The Bible says, **"Therefore put on God's complete armor, that you may be able to resist *and* stand your ground on the evil day [of danger], and, having done all [the crisis demands], to stand [firmly in your place]."** (Ephesians 6:13, Amplified)

So, our scripture says, "I shall not be moved." Does it mean David is not changing condos this weekend? No. It means that no matter WHAT he sees with his eyes (in this physical realm), he shall not be moved off point – off his beliefs that God is his fortress, his strong tower, his salvation, his deliverer, his vindicator, his provider, his healer, and all the other things that God was to him – and is to us! His Power is in his stability, and his stability is God. And so is YOURS!

There is POWER in your belief system. It gives you structure, and structure is strength. You can build on the framework of your belief system. You can build a healthy life, strong and healthy relationships and healthy ministries. I heard once that if you don't stand for something, you'll fall for anything! I believe that is true, especially with our next generation.

If you don't know what your beliefs are, you are easily moved by whatever comes your way. If temptation comes and you grow weary of one type of pleasure, you will simply move on to the next. If you get tired of one boyfriend (or husband) and you are tempted, you will simply move on to the next. That is the way of the destroyer, the enemy that comes to kill, steal and destroy (John 10:10).

However, if you are locked into your beliefs as a Christian, you can take a stand against the enemy and his wiles. Put on your armor, so that when that day comes, and you have done ALL that you are able to do, that you can STAND. You shall not be moved.

"He who dwells in the secret place of the Most High shall remain stable *and* fixed under the shadow of the Almighty [Whose power no foe can withstand]. I will say of the Lord, He is my Refuge and my Fortress, my God; on Him I lean *and* rely, *and* in Him I [confidently] trust!" (Psalm 91:1-2)

Perhaps you or someone you know are in financial straits, have lost a job, your savings in this economy or it may even appear that you are losing your home or your vehicle. Do not be moved! The bible says in Philippians 4:19, **"And my God will liberally supply (fill to the full) your every need according to His riches in glory in Christ Jesus."**

Please note: the verse says "according to HIS riches in Glory", not yours. I'd rather depend on His riches and not on my own! All the cattle on a thousand hillsides are His, all the silver is His, and all the gold is His, and He is your Father. The fullness of the earth and everything in it is His. It's ALL His. Every bit of it. Everything in Heaven and on Earth is His. And He's your Dad!

Good Dads take care of their children. And He is the best.

Depend on His Word. Stand on His Word. Do not be moved!

There is Power in it.

CHAPTER 6:

THEREFORE MY HEART IS GLAD AND
MY GLORY [MY INNER SELF] REJOICES

Power is Fun!

There is Power in being glad and rejoicing in the Lord.
Do a word-search for "JOY" with an Amplified Bible
and your results will be all about food and music! The
Lord is all about feasting and dancing and singing.
God loves celebrations! "And be not grieved *and*
depressed, for the **joy** of the Lord is your strength *and*
stronghold." (Neh. 8:10, Amplified)

PLEASE NOTE: We are not talking about HAPPY here.
Happy is a state of mind, an emotion, a feeling. We do
not walk by FEELINGS, we walk by FAITH! Faith gives

us JOY! And that is what we are talking about here, the JOY that comes with being a spiritual lightning rod, connected to the Father of Lights!

All of the following scriptures are about joy, and rejoicing, all from the Amplified. There are so many scriptures about joy it could fill another entire book! God WANTS us to be joyful, glad, rejoice and enjoy our lives. Let your inner self rejoice!

And have FUN!

"...**because the Lord your God will bless you in all your produce and in all the works of your hands, so that you will be altogether joyful**." (Deut 16:15) God wants to bless us so that we have much! He blesses us with provision, blesses us with food and blesses our businesses so that we are a joyful, smiling bunch of folks. People are attracted to smiling people! Who wants to hang out with a bunch of broke sour-pusses? Get rid of the POVERTY MENTALITY! God wants you to be blessed and prosperous. And Joyful!

"**All the people followed him; they played on pipes and rejoiced greatly, so that the earth [resounded] with the joyful sound.**" (1Kings 1:40) Again, music. God LOVES music! He loves Music so much that He created the Music Minister to end ALL Music Ministers, the one who turned against Him, satan. God just loves music so much He has given us that same love for it in our very DNA. He wants US to enjoy it as much as He does, so He gives us ample opportunity to worship and praise, sing and dance and have fun! And EAT!

"**On the eighth day he sent the people away; they blessed the king and went to their tents with greatest joy and gratitude for all the goodness the**

Lord had shown to David His servant and Israel His people." (1Kings 8:66) The Lord has given us great joy over His goodness. Has the Lord been good to you? He sure has been good to me! It gives me great joy when God is good to me, because it means He has been thinking of me and planning something special just for me! These blessings of the Lord don't just happen! God has to line up all the people and all the events that must transpire for that particular "goodie" to take place!

Think about the last time you found money! Remember in Matthew 17 when Jesus told Peter to go fishing and take the first fish that comes up? In its mouth would be a gold coin! How many events must have transpired in EXACTLY THE RIGHT ORDER AT EXACTLY THE RIGHT TIME for that fish to have a gold coin in its mouth? First, the fisherman that lost the money would have to be born at the right moment. Then the fishing company would need to be formed. This fisherman would then have to be hired on with that company. Then he would have to make his paycheck, cash it, have some money to buy the lures and the poles and his fishing license. Then he would be made to stand up on his boat, lose his balance enough to either fall out of the boat or lose the bag that held the gold coins. And what caused him to lose his balance, God?

At any rate, the fish would have to be hatched at just the right time to be hungry at the exact moment that fisherman would lose his coin/s, swim by at just the right moment and take a bite out of that coin bag!

Now, hang on! Peter would have to be on the water at exactly the right moment to catch that particular fish that had gone after the gold coin! If God wasn't in control, how would ALL of this have happened to make Jesus' one sentence that he said to Peter come true?

And just think, every single blessing of the Lord has to work in exactly this same way! Every time He has blessed you, how many hundreds of events had to come to pass for you to receive your blessing? Even as simple as finding a $20 bill on the ground outside a store? First, the person that lost the money had to be born, then....

"Also those who were near them from as far as Issachar, Zebulun, and Naphtali brought food on donkeys, camels, mules, and oxen, abundant supplies of meal, cakes of figs, bunches of raisins, wine, oil, oxen, and sheep, for there was joy in Israel." (1 Chron. 12:40) Again with the food! This time there is so much it takes CAMEL trains to transport it! Joy! Joy! Joy! It's a magnet for people with stuff and everybody LOVES a party! There is power in Joy! So enjoy the party!

"Honor and majesty are [found] in His presence; strength and joy are [found] in His sanctuary." (1Chron 16:27) Aha! Here's a scripture about the presence of the Lord bringing us Joy. There is joy in the presence of the Lord. "...**in your presence there is fullness of joy; at your right hand are pleasures forevermore.**" (Psalm 16:11) There is joy in the presence of the Lord, fullness of joy. Unspeakable joy. Who can be mad or anything other than joyful, reverent, content and peaceful in the presence of the Lord? (There is that *right hand of power* thing again!)

"Then [Ezra] told them, Go your way, eat the fat, drink the sweet drink, and send portions to him for whom nothing is prepared; for this day is holy to our Lord. And be not grieved *and* depressed, for

the joy of the Lord is your strength *and* stronghold." (Neh. 8:10) These Israelites must have been a FAT breed of people, with all the feasting and drinking and dancing and singing that they did!

But in another section of the Word it says, **"All the Fat is the Lord's!"** (Leviticus 3:16)

HA!

Can you just imagine how amazing Heaven will be? If the earth is just a type and shadow of Heaven, and here we get to eat, drink and be merry, party and fellowship and dance and worship the King of Kings...can you just imagine what it will be like for all eternity?

Heavenly!

EDIE BAYER

CHAPTER 7

MY BODY TOO SHALL REST *AND*
CONFIDENTLY DWELL IN SAFETY

There is POWER in rest.

Have you ever had to work the next day after being up
really, really late at night? Maybe with only a couple
of hours sleep, or maybe none at all? As a younger
person I routinely stayed up late at night and went to
work the next day. Now, as a more mature person (I
didn't say OLD!) it is a lot harder to accomplish that
same act. Why? Because REST gives us strength, and
strength gives us POWER. Without power it's
impossible to accomplish the tasks that need to be

done every day. I need my physical rest and I am sure you do, too.

The Lord states in this verse that we SHALL REST and dwell in safety. If you do not feel that you are safe and secure – whether financially, physically or relationally --- or you KNOW you are not, you will not be able to sleep at night. You will either be thinking about your lack of safety and security or watching out to try to stay safe. Even when you are able to go to sleep your subconscious will still be trying to work it all out.

As an example, my Mom and Dad recently discovered a water leak under their house. They don't know how long it's been leaking. My Mother said their water bill was $20.00 higher last month than it has been. She admitted she actually lost sleep over the water bill!

That is worry. Nothing is more exhausting and less profitable than being worried. Worry is exhausting because it eats up hours and energy, doing nothing! Worry is an anxious word; it means to be concerned or nervous. Being nervous makes a person tired! You use up a lot of adrenaline, and it throws your entire body out of whack.

Psalm 16 tells us that we can rest and **_confidently_** dwell in safety. Psalm 91 reiterates this and expounds upon it. It states that we are safe from the fowler's snare. When you are His you are safe, sound and secure. You dwell in safety and security. You can rest in the knowledge that you are safe.

Read Psalm 91 closely, slowly, paying close attention to how much God talks about your safety and security:

Psalm 91 (Amplified)

[1] He who dwells in the secret place of the Most High shall remain stable *and* fixed under the shadow of the Almighty [Whose power no foe can withstand].

[2] I will say of the Lord, He is my Refuge and my Fortress, my God; on Him I lean *and* rely, *and* in Him I [confidently] trust!

[3] For [then] He will deliver you from the snare of the fowler and from the deadly pestilence. [4] [Then] He will cover you with His pinions, and under His wings shall you trust *and* find refuge; His truth *and* His faithfulness are a shield and a buckler.

[5] You shall not be afraid of the terror of the night, nor of the arrow (the evil plots and slanders of the wicked) that flies by day,

[6] Nor of the pestilence that stalks in darkness, nor of the destruction *and* sudden death that surprise *and* lay waste at noonday.

[7] A thousand may fall at your side, and ten thousand at your right hand, but it shall not come near you.

[8] Only a spectator shall you be [yourself inaccessible in the secret place of the Most High] as you witness the reward of the wicked.

[9] Because you have made the Lord your refuge, and the Most High your dwelling place,

[10] There shall no evil befall you, nor any plague *or* calamity come near your tent.

[11] For He will give His angels [especial] charge over you to accompany *and* defend *and* preserve you in all your ways [of obedience and service].

[12] They shall bear you up on their hands, lest you dash your foot against a stone.

[13] You shall tread upon the lion and adder; the young lion and the serpent shall you trample underfoot.

[14] Because he has set his love upon Me, therefore will I deliver him; I will set him on high, because

**he knows *and* understands My name [has a
personal knowledge of My mercy, love, and
kindness—trusts and relies on Me, knowing I will
never forsake him, no, never].
15 He shall call upon Me, and I will answer him; I
will be with him in trouble, I will deliver him and
honor him.
16 With long life will I satisfy him and show him My
salvation.**

BUT...because God is an "If/Then" God, meaning that
His Word continually says, "IF you do something,
THEN I will respond (like this)", it means that YOU
must make the first move. YOU must "...dwell in the
secret place of the Most High".

That takes a commitment on your part. It is NOT for
the weak at heart! I started out by saying that if you
are His, you are safe, sound and secure. That means
what it says....that you are His.

That means you live in His Kingdom, where He is King
and He calls the shots! You walk under His Lordship.
You do what He says. You obey the still, small voice.
You pray, and fast. You worship the One, True King.
You live for Him and you are willing to die for Him.
Your flesh dies to itself for Him, that's for sure. You're
the one that must kill it.

He is your Father. You are called to an intimate
relationship with Him. Dwelling in the Secret Place of
the Most High is not for casual church-goers. This is a
call of deep to deep.

If you are not ready for this kind of commitment, it's
ok. He will wait. He is your bride groom.

Will He still love you? Absolutely. But it cannot be a one-sided bargain with God providing all the benefits and you doing whatever you want with whomever you want. It will be activated once you commit to the Lord your life, your plans, your desires, your relationships, your heart. He wants everything. He wants it all.

As I said, it is not for the weak. It is not for those who are pew warmers, or only attending church on holidays, or those who are in a "Sunday Social Club". His protection is for those who WANT a relationship with Him. Because He desperately wants one with you.

So much so that He died on the cross for it.

Of course, there are a LOT of added extra benefits once you cross-over into a full blown relationship with Jesus. It's like the marriage relationship. Once you are married (in a community property state, which our marriage with our Lord is!) you are entitled to half of EVERYTHING. So, once you are married, you own ½ of the house, ½ of the car, and are responsible for ½ of all that goes with it, as well.

In the book of Esther, it says, **"What will you have, Queen Esther? What is your request? It shall be given you, even to the half of the kingdom."** (Esther 5:3, Amp.)

It is the same with the marriage to the Lamb of God. The Bible says, **"Bless (affectionately, gratefully praise) the Lord, O my soul, and forget not [one of] all His benefits."** (Psalm 103:2, Amplified)

You get it all, but you have responsibilities that go with it, too. You must be committed to the relationship.

So, the question is this – Are you God's? Are you a Son or a Daughter of the Most High God? A Son or a Daughter has an intimate relationship with Him, they know their identity is in Christ, and they know their Dad. They do His will, and they have laid down their life for Him.

But let's start with the basics. Are you 'Saved'? If you died tonight in your sleep, are you 100% sure you would go to heaven? If there is even a shadow of a doubt, PLEASE say the prayer below.

If you are reading this book, you are probably 'Saved', but let's just make sure, ok? Read this prayer out loud:

"Dear Lord Jesus,

I know I am a sinner, and I ask for your forgiveness. I believe you died for my sins and rose from the dead. I trust and follow you as my Lord and Savior. Guide my life and help me to do your will.

In your name, amen."

That is step one. You are now a member of the family of God, and the Angels are rejoicing in Heaven!

Now for step two – Get filled with the Holy Spirit! If you need help with this, please contact your Pastor, or call, text, Facebook or email Edie Bayer or Kingdom Promoters. We'll be happy to help you get baptized with the Holy Spirit and get your prayer language, as well.

Then the next step is the longest one. It will take you the rest of your life! It will be a process, so don't get discouraged. Just keep walking forward and it will be a good thing, for you, your family and for your life.

If you have already done #1 and #2, and you are working on #3 and need assistance, prayer or have questions, please contact us at Kingdom Promoters. Use the contact information in the Biography section of the book, or visit our webpage, www.KingdomPromoters.org.

Then you will rest and dwell in confidence – Forever!

Endnotes:

(1) Wikipedia, Hebrew Numerals, Calculations:
http://en.wikipedia.org/wiki/Hebrew_numerals

(2) WordCentral.com
http://www.wordcentral.com/cgi-
bin/student?book=Student&va=psalm

(3) Interpreting the Symbols and Types, Kevin J.
Conner. "Hand", page 147

(4) http://whatthebiblesays.info/TheRightHandofGod.html

ABOUT THE AUTHOR

Edie Bayer's primary focus is to promote and advance the Kingdom of God by helping people to hear and recognize the voice of the Lord, and then act upon it. Edie has served with international ministers Joan Hunter and Paulette Reed as well as Darren Canning and Dr. Judy Laird. Edie ministers as a Preacher and Prophet of God. She is an author, a speaker and itinerant minister.

Edie and her husband Darryl formed Kingdom Promoters (www.KingdomPromoters.org), to help further God's Kingdom by acting as an incubator to assist fledgling ministries in their start-up stages. Kingdom Promoters also hosts itinerant speakers and travelling ministers such as Dr. Linda Smith and Apostle William Dillon, as well as author Carol Sewell, among others.

Edie and Darryl reside on a small homestead north of the Houston area. They raise chickens, ducks, quail and rabbits and have three cats. Edie has two children and three grandchildren.

You may reach Edie and Darryl at their website, www.KingdomPromoters.org and www.TexasBrass.com

Darryl Bayer has many CD's available on CDBaby.com and Amazon.com. You can find videos of them on YouTube.com

You may also read and sign up for Edie's blog, http://ediebear1.wordpress.com .

You may also wish to email Edie, ediebear1@gmail.com

Darryl and Edie are available to play, preach and prophesy at your church, ladies group or other event. Contact us!

Other titles by Edie Bayer:
1. Spiritual Espionage, Going Undercover for the Kingdom of God
2. Power Thieves, 7-Spirits that Steal Your Power and How to Get it Back!
3. Spiritual Lightning Rods, Connected to the Father of Lights
Watch for new book and music releases coming soon!

Made in the USA
Las Vegas, NV
13 February 2022

43888536R00028